Jazz Piano Basics

Encore

17 Original Solos to Enhance Your Jazzabilities
BY ERIC BAUMGARTNER

Several pieces in this collection first appeared in *Jazz Connection* and *Jazzabilities*. The versions within have been revised by the composer, each designed to increase musical appeal and to match the flow and scope of *Jazz Piano Basics*.

PLAYBACK+
Speed • Pitch • Balance • Loop

To access audio, visit:
www.halleonard.com/mylibrary

Enter Code
2007-0762-2048-4284

ISBN 978-1-5400-4057-2

WILLIS MUSIC

EXCLUSIVELY DISTRIBUTED BY

Hal•Leonard®

Visit Hal Leonard Online at
www.halleonard.com

World headquarters, contact:
Hal Leonard
7777 West Bluemound Road
Milwaukee, WI 53213
Email: info@halleonard.com

In Europe, contact:
Hal Leonard Europe Limited
42 Wigmore Street
Marylebone, London, W1U 2RY
Email: info@halleonardeurope.com

In Australia, contact:
Hal Leonard Australia Pty. Ltd.
4 Lentara Court
Cheltenham, Victoria, 3192 Australia
Email: info@halleonard.com.au

Preface

In assembling this collection my goal was to create a broad musical canvas, featuring pieces in a wide variety of moods and styles, including styles beyond traditional jazz. The reason for this eclectic mix is because the elements we most closely associate with jazz music—syncopated rhythms, swing, bluesy melodies, sophisticated harmonies—are by no means *exclusive* to jazz music! The influence of jazz is immense. Elements of jazz are present, to varying degrees, in every popular musical style of today. Musicians with a jazz education, therefore, often have a distinct advantage when venturing into different styles. Look for these jazzy elements as you explore the pieces within *Encore*, whether in the playful bounce of "Fol-de-rol," the smooth Caribbean groove of "Island Breeze," or in the up-tempo swing of "Jumpin' with Mr. Jordan." For specific details on each piece be sure to check out the Performance Notes located near the end of the book. Enjoy!

Eric Baumgartner

Guide

Jazz Piano Basics. This collection is a companion to the two-volume series, *Jazz Piano Basics*, a method that presents the fundamentals of jazz in a logical and accessible fashion. Each piece within *Encore* is designed to reinforce a concept or technique in *Jazz Piano Basics*. You may choose to work on these pieces in tandem with *Jazz Piano Basics* or play them independently of any series and simply enjoy them as fun solos.

Chord Symbols. The pieces corresponding with Book 2 of *Jazz Piano Basics* (also referred to as JPB) contain chord symbols. Each symbol acts as a summary of the harmony present at that particular point within the piece. Every chord (and symbol) employed in *Encore* is introduced and explored in JPB2. You needn't necessarily have studied the chords and their symbols in order to master these pieces. They are fully notated and require no further construction or improvisation. You may approach them as you would any piece in your repertoire. However, a good understanding of harmony provides valuable insight into the process of composing and arranging. This in turn allows one to learn pieces more efficiently and accurately. Consider returning to any piece at a later point (after additional experience with harmony) to appreciate its construction more fully.

Audio Tracks. Each piece has two audio tracks. The first contains a recorded version of the piece to a backing track and is labeled "Practice." The second contains only the backing track and is labeled "Performance." The Practice track is ideal to play along with while you are gaining confidence in the piece but would still like the support of a recorded piano part. It is also useful as an audio reference when faced with a new and challenging rhythm. The Performance track is perfect when you are ready to tackle the exercise without a safety net! Put in sufficient time to master the rhythm and prepare the piece (or section) before attempting to play along with either track.

The Practice and Performance tracks for each piece are set to the same tempo. If you find a tempo too brisk, the *Playback+* function in MyLibrary (**www.halleonard.com/mylibrary**) allows you to adjust the tempo. This feature is common to other media players as well. Explore different tempi to find the optimal practice speed for each piece. *Playback+* also allows you to set loop points for repetition of challenging (or fun!) measures.

Contents

4 Calypso Carnival

6 Easy Does It

8 Funkasaurus

10 Cool It!

11 A Swing Thing

12 The Brazilian Bop

14 Mellow Mood

16 Fol-de-rol

18 Main at Midnight

20 Out on a Limbo

22 Burgundy Street Blues

24 Berry Blue Jam

26 Island Breeze

28 Jumpin' with Mr. Jordan

30 Reflection

32 Tango Up in Blue

34 Bossa Rio

37 PERFORMANCE NOTES

Calypso Carnival

Eric Baumgartner

Easy Does It

Eric Baumgartner

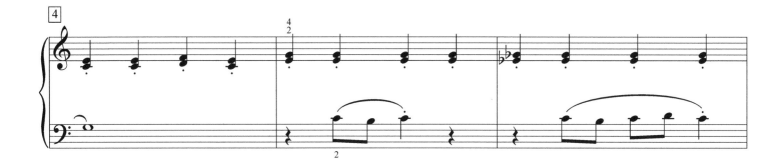

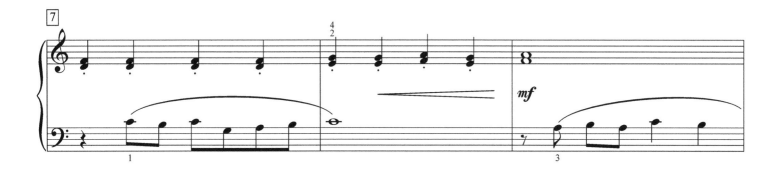

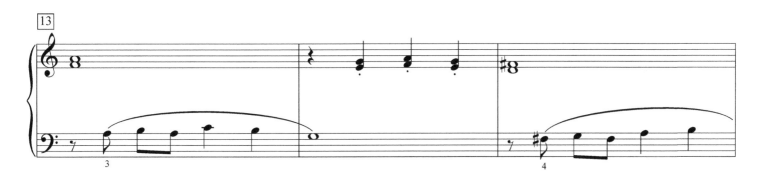

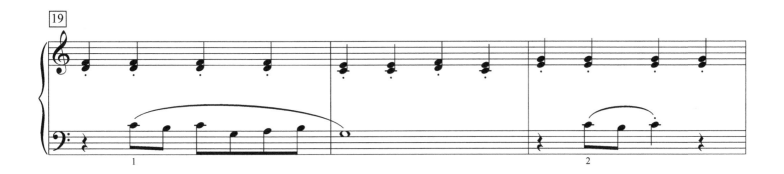

Funkasaurus

Eric Baumgartner

Moving steadily (with attitude!)

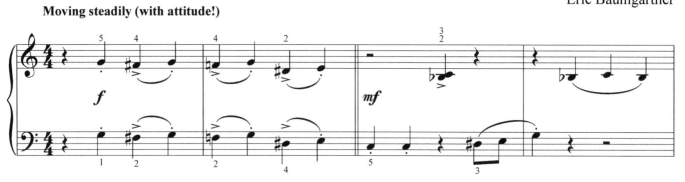

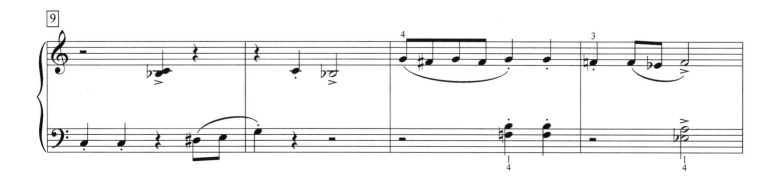

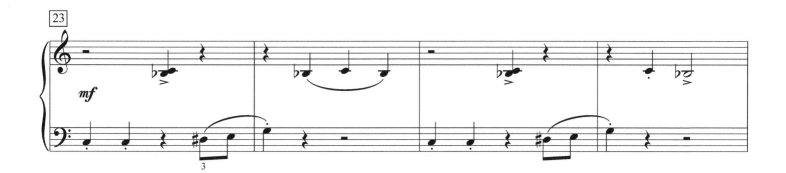

Cool It!

Eric Baumgartner

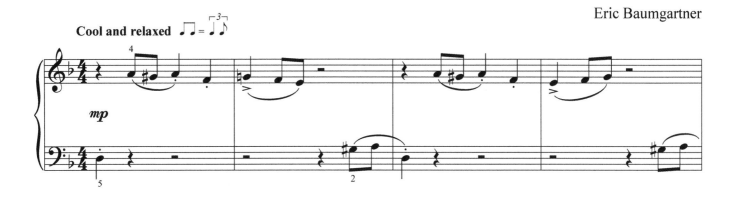

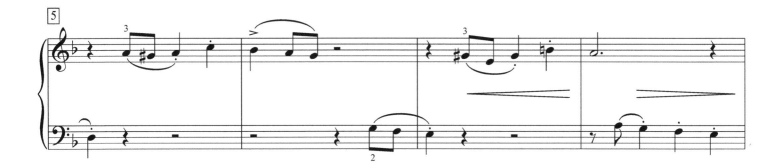

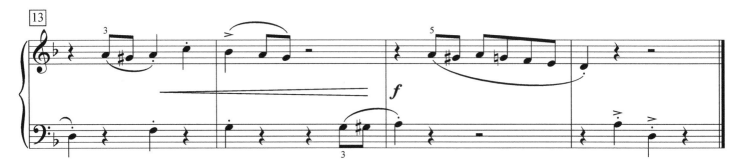

A Swing Thing

Eric Baumgartner

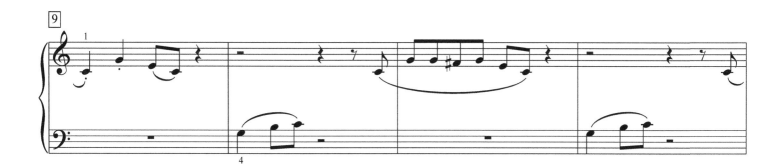

The Brazilian Bop

Eric Baumgartner

Quickly, with excitement

Mellow Mood

Eric Baumgartner

Fol-de-rol

Eric Baumgartner

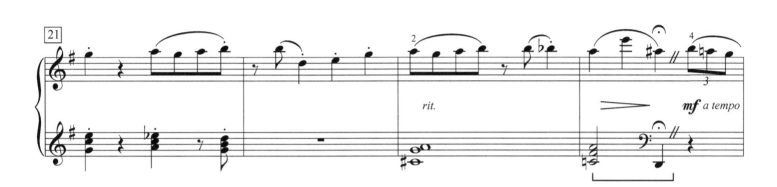

Main at Midnight

Eric Baumgartner

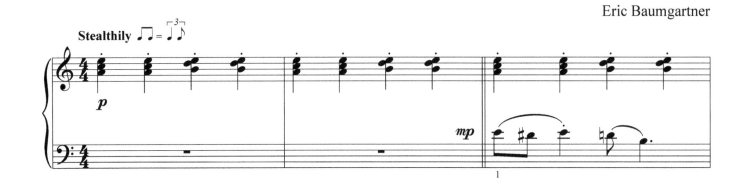

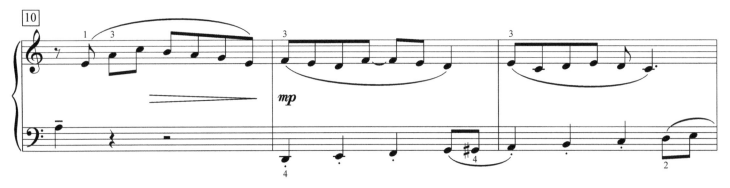

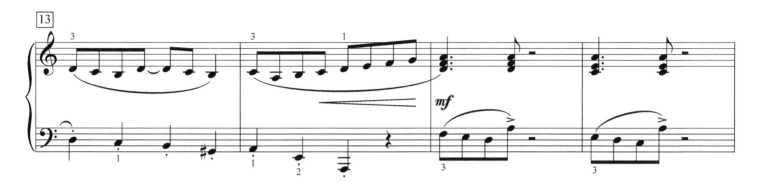

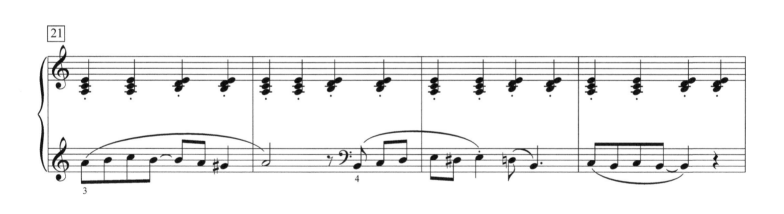

Out on a Limbo

Eric Baumgartner

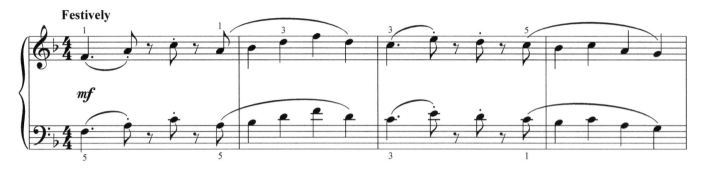

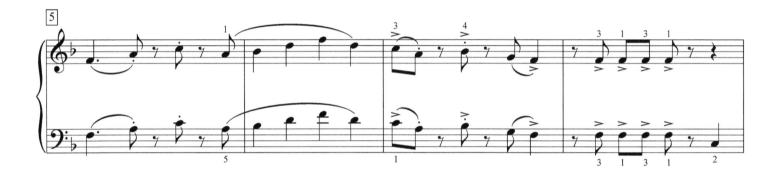

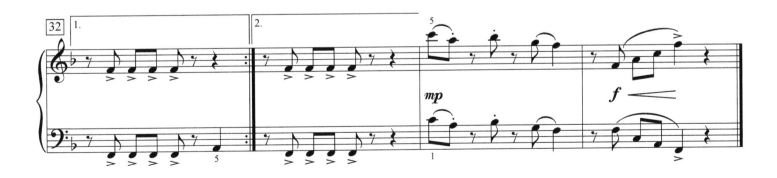

Burgundy Street Blues

Eric Baumgartner

Bluesy, unhurried

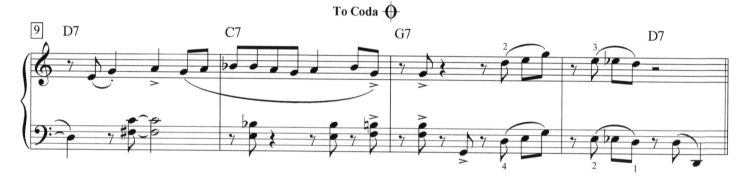

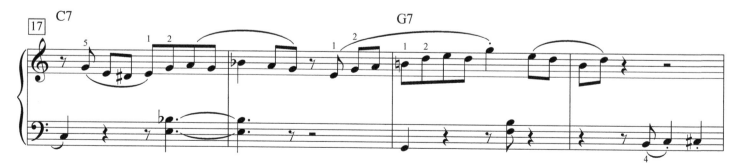

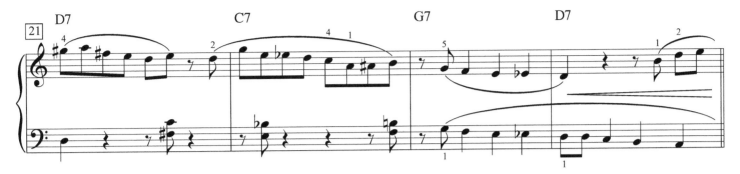

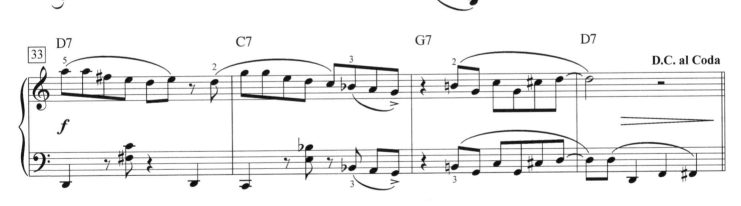

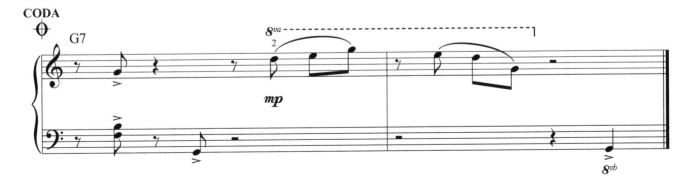

Berry Blue Jam

Eric Baumgartner

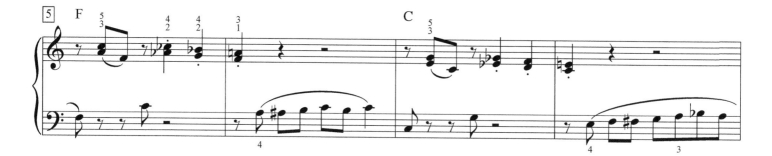

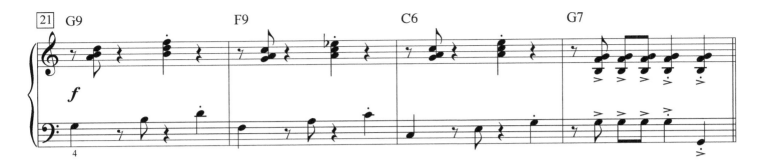

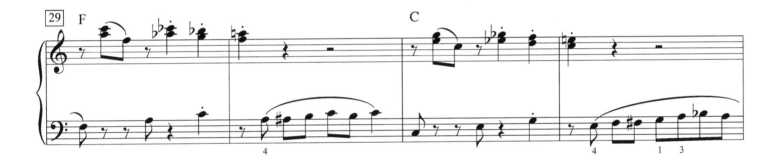

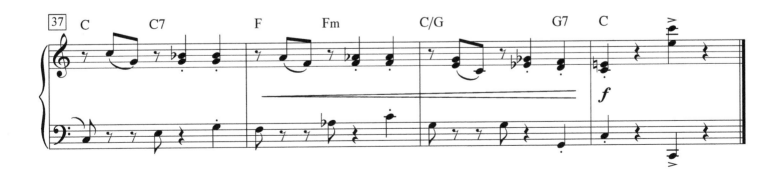

Island Breeze

Eric Baumgartner

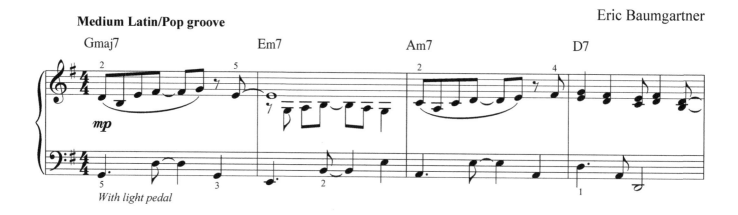

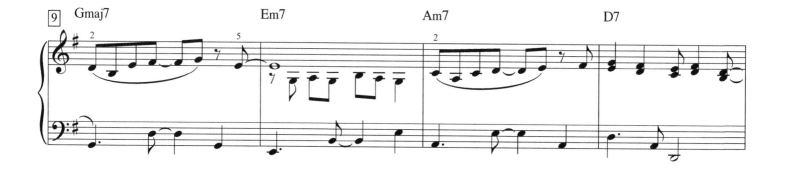

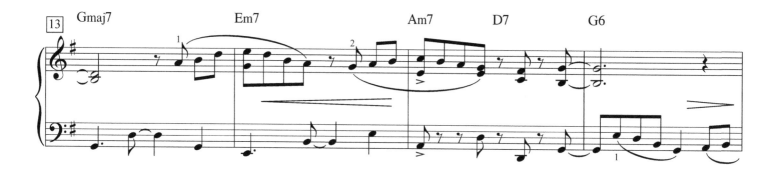

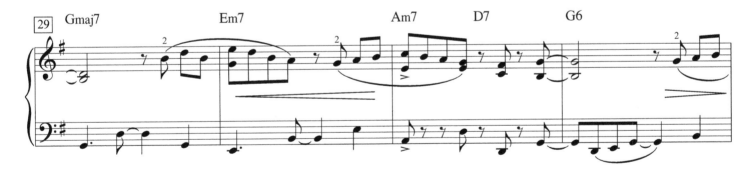

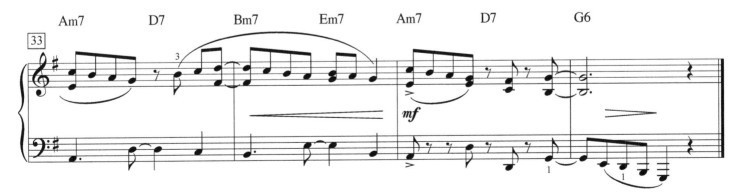

Jumpin' with Mr. Jordan

Eric Baumgartner

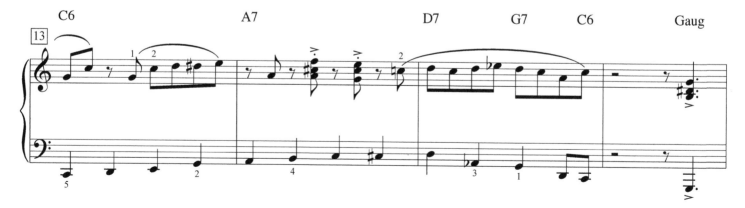

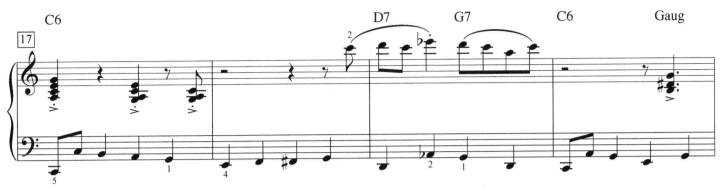

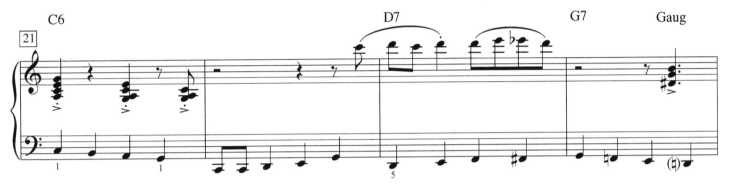

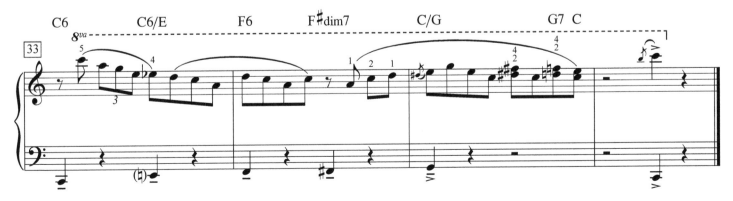

Reflection

Eric Baumgartner

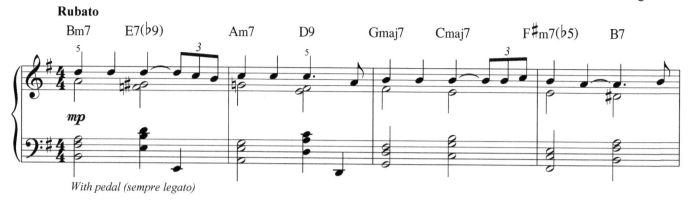

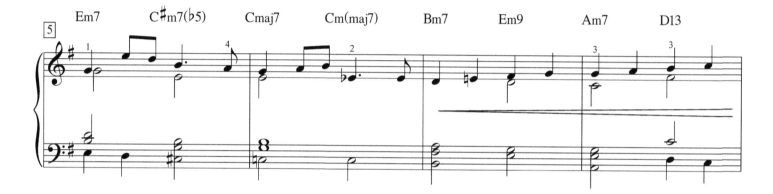

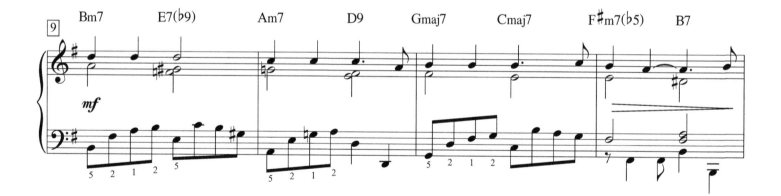

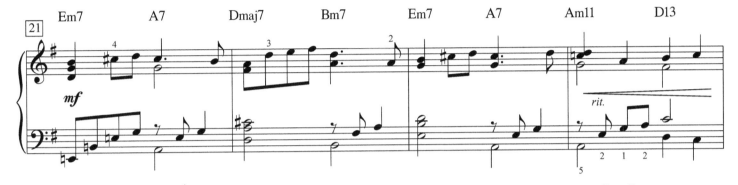

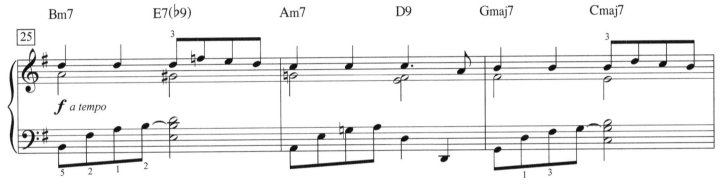

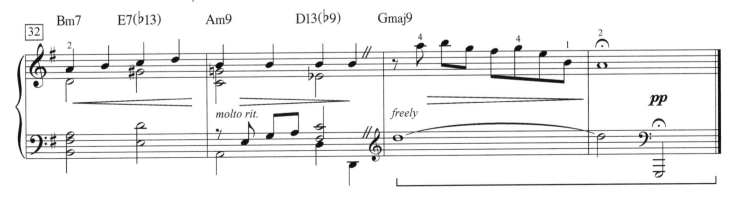

Tango Up in Blue

Eric Baumgartner

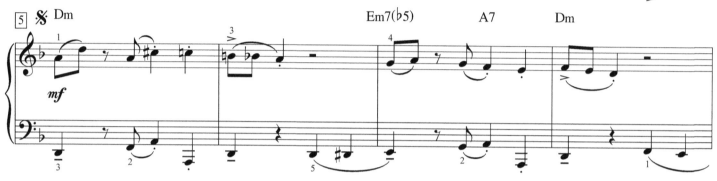

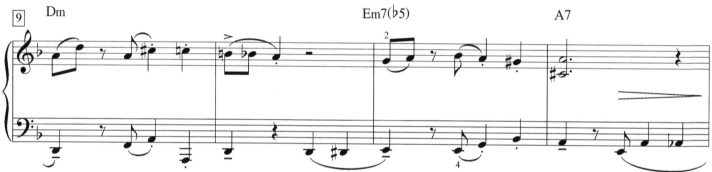

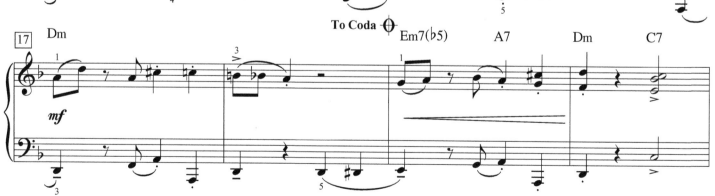

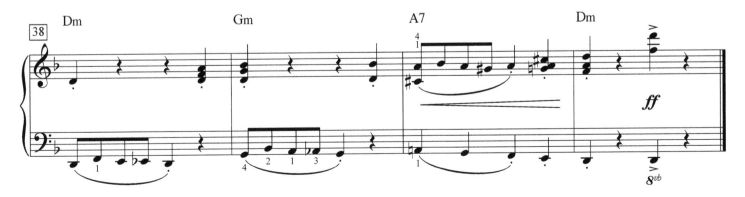

Bossa Rio

Eric Baumgartner

Briskly, with authority

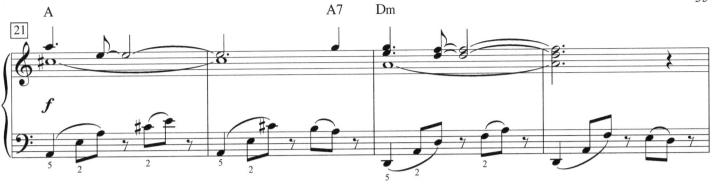

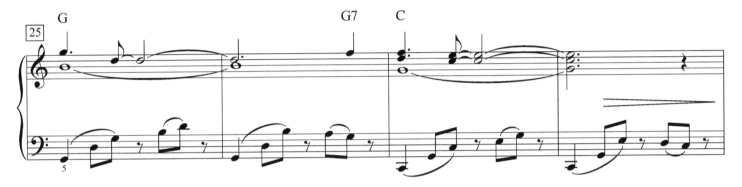

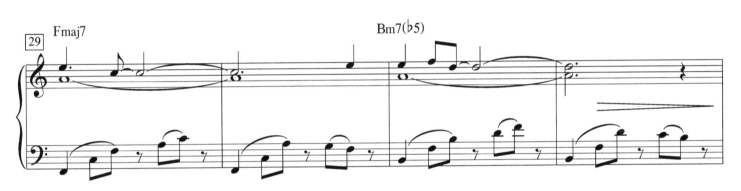

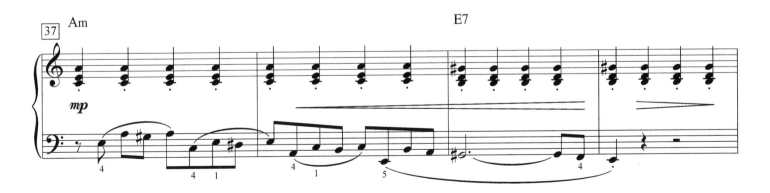

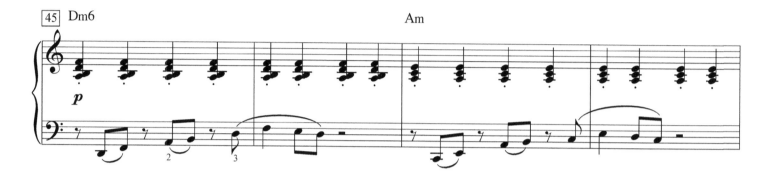

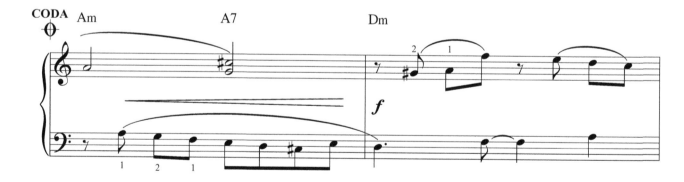

Performance Notes

Calypso Carnival
Use with *Jazz Piano Basics*, Book 1 (JPB1), Chapter 1 (Introductory Exercises).
This is a revised version of a piece that first appeared in *Jazz Connection*, Book 1.

Take a moment to look at the rhythms of this fun, festive piece. Despite its length, notice that a few unique rhythmic patterns are repeated over and over. This is common in all musical styles. Memorize each new pattern by clapping and counting it. This will help you learn the piece accurately and with greater efficiency. Keep the staccato notes crisp and the accented notes strong. Attention to detail will lead to a confident, crowd-pleasing performance!

Easy Does It
Use with JPB1, Chapter 1 (Introductory Exercises).
This is a revised version of a piece that first appeared in *Jazz Connection*, Book 1.

There's a hint of the blues in this gentle pop piece. You'll hear it in the first four measures of the right hand—a series of thirds that forms a classic descending blues pattern. Yet this is not the melody, it's the accompaniment. Keep it steady in support of the left-hand melody. Experiment with the dynamics of the melody, adding crescendo and diminuendo within phrases for expression.

Funkasaurus
Use with JPB1, Chapter 1 (Introductory Exercises).
This is a revised version of a piece that first appeared in *Jazz Connection*, Book 1.

You'll notice a bunch of sharps, flats, and naturals throughout "Funkasaurus." These altered tones produce a distinctive bluesy sound that helps make this piece so funky and fun to play! Work on one phrase at a time. Carefully compare each new phrase to the previous one to see how they differ. Once all the patterns are firmly in your fingers, increase the tempo bit by bit. Your goal is to play it fast enough that it can be felt "in two" (listen to the audio).

Cool It!
Use with JPB1, Chapter 2 (Swing It!).
This piece first appeared in *Jazzabilitie*s, Book 1.

This is the first of many pieces in this collection to use swung eighth notes, played in "long-short" pairs. If you are new to the concept of *swing*, listen to the audio tracks for reference. It shouldn't take you long to get the feel of it. The practice of swinging the eighths is most closely associated with jazz, but it's common in much of contemporary music. You'll find examples of swung eighth notes in styles like hip hop, country, Broadway, pop and rock music.

A Swing Thing
Use with JPB1, Chapter 3 (Pickup Notes).
This is a revised version of a piece that first appeared in *Jazz Connection*, Book 1.

The challenge in this short, swung piece (unlike in "Cool It!") is that many of the phrases begin, not on the quarter-note beats, but on the "ands" between them. In other words they start on the *short* eighth notes, not the *long* ones. As always, think rhythm first. Lock into a slow and steady swing pulse before clapping and counting out the rhythms. Listen also to the audio tracks for help with tricky rhythms.

The Brazilian Bop
Use with JPB1, Chapter 4 (Latin Jazz).
This is a revised version of a piece that first appeared in *Jazz Connection*, Book 1.

Latin jazz often uses syncopated rhythms but, unlike swing, the eighth notes are played straight. "The Brazilian Bop" uses many chromatic passages (moving up or down by half steps). These phrases may feel a little awkward and unfamiliar at first. Take extra care to use the suggested fingering. This will help you to efficiently learn each new phrase. When ready, challenge yourself to play the piece at a fast tempo. A brisk speed helps in unleashing the excitement and energy of the Latin jazz style.

Mellow Mood
Use with JPB1, Chapter 6 (Classic & Cool).
This piece first appeared in *Jazz Connection*, Book 2.

The rhythms here are fairly simple overall, with only a few syncopated spots. However, the melodic and harmonic components are tricky. Almost every measure contains accidentals, signaling the use of bluesy melodic notes and harmonies borrowed from outside the key of C. Keep the tempo relaxed and bluesy (swinging the eighths) and be consistent in your fingering.

Fol-de-rol
Use with JPB1, Chapter 8 (The Major Pentatonic Scale).

The right-hand melodic phrases in this playful piece consist of notes from the G Major pentatonic scale. Take a moment to compare each phrase to the scale. This will help you to see more clearly the construction and shape of each phrase. The jazzy chords (found in measures 3 and 4, etc.) are similar to those common in big band swing. Keep them light, yet crisp and confident. Feel free to explore different tempi, although the humor and playful nature of this piece may best be realized at faster speeds.

Main at Midnight
Use after JPB1.
This is a revised version of a piece that first appeared in *Jazz Connection*, Book 2.

For much of this solo, the left hand provides the melody while the right accompanies. This type of role reversal can be a challenge, particularly with syncopated swing rhythms! Bring out the left-hand melody while keeping the right hand steady and supportive. Notice that the melody switches to the right hand for much of the middle section (starting in m. 10). Now it's time to bring out the right hand as the left plays a more traditional jazz bass line. Keep the tempo relaxed, with a loose swing feel throughout.

Out on a Limbo
Use after JPB1.
This piece first appeared in *Jazz Connection*, Book 3.

This festive piece is in the Caribbean style. Caribbean rhythms are often syncopated and played with straight eighth notes, similar to Latin jazz. The chordal harmonies tend to be simple and the tonality brightly major. The hands play in octave unison for the opening section; the left hand then switches to an independent bass line. Carefully work out each measure to see how the parts align. Some measures will be trickier than others! Be patient, and lock into a slow, steady eighth-note pulse. Your goal: gain the control and confidence to play at a lively pace.

Burgundy Street Blues
Use with *Jazz Piano Basics*, Book 2 (JPB2), Chapter 3 (The 12-Bar Blues).

"Burgundy Street Blues" is written in the classic 12-bar blues style. It uses I, IV, and V chords from the key of G, all modified (as is customary in the blues) to dominant sevenths. Note the use of double bar lines. Each one signals the end of a 12-bar cycle or "chorus." The opening melody, or "head," uses notes from the G Major blues scale. The left-hand accompaniment employs a combination of 2-note chordal voicings, root notes, and melodic "fills" throughout.

[NOTE: This blues in G does not include a key signature. This was done for clarity since the blues typically uses notes altered from the major scale. However, it is common for blues pieces to use major key signatures with the appropriate accidentals added.]

Berry Blue Jam
Use with JPB2, Chapter 4 (Classic Blues Licks).
This is a revised version of a piece that first appeared in *Jazz Connection*, Book 2.

"Berry Blue Jam" is built almost entirely upon classic harmonic and melodic blues licks. Explore the shape of each lick to see how it relates to the chord symbol. Like the previous piece, "Jam" uses the 12-bar blues form, this time in C. There are three choruses followed by a 4-measure coda or "tag." Strive for broad contrasts in dynamics, and experiment with accents on different notes for variety.

Island Breeze
Use with JPB2, Chapter 5 (Playing in Major Keys).

Take a look at the notes of this piece. Notice that there are no accidentals! This signals that the piece is entirely *diatonic*, meaning it consists only of notes derived from its key (G Major). The I through vi chords in the key of G provide all the harmonic content. You may find a similar challenge here as with "Out on a Limbo" when combining the hands: both pieces are in a Caribbean style and feature an independent bass alongside a syncopated melody. However, "Island Breeze" is meant to be played at a slower tempo and should have a more mellow feel.

Jumpin' with Mr. Jordan
Use with JPB2, Chapter 7 (Walking Bass).

This piece is a tribute to the songwriter and bandleader, Louis Jordan. He was one of the most successful artists of the swing, boogie-woogie, and "jump" eras of the 1940s and 50s. His music was often up-tempo and fused with infectious swing rhythms and humor. "Jumpin' with Mr. Jordan" employs many of the techniques found in Jordan's music and his contemporaries. The arrangement is anchored by the left hand playing a steady "walking" bass throughout. The right hand has double duty; first, the single-line melody. Picture it being sung (or "scatted" with nonsense syllables) or played by saxophone or trumpet. Second, the chord hits. These short accented hits (or "stabs") are usually played by a group of horns or woodwinds in between the melodic phrases. Check out Mr. Jordan's music for inspiration: "Caldonia," "Choo Choo Ch'Boogie," and "Ain't Nobody Here but Us Chickens" are all fine places to start.

Reflection
Use with JPB2, Chapter 9 (Extended Chords).

"Reflection" is modeled after the beautiful jazz standards of the 1930s and 40s. The main bodies of these songs (known as *choruses*) typically consisted of four 8-measure sections (AABA) totaling 32 measures in length. The standards of this period (particularly the slow songs, or "ballads") were known for their harmonic complexity. Chords often contained extensions (tones beyond the seventh) and shifted in and out of the home key with grace and fluidity. Notable composers of this era included George Gershwin, Harold Arlen, and Jerome Kern. Classic examples of this style and form include "Over the Rainbow," "Misty," and "Body and Soul."

The chords are often spread between the hands. The challenge for the right hand is to bring out the melody while sustaining the chord tones lightly underneath. Use good fingering. Strive to play as legato as possible with the fingers (rather than relying on the pedal). The *rubato* marking means that you should gently "push and pull" the tempo for dramatic emphasis. The audio tracks demonstrate this, but the effect is purposely subtle to make it easier when playing along. Feel free to explore wider tempo variations when playing on your own.

Tango Up in Blue
Use with JPB2, Chapter 10 (Playing in Minor Keys).
This is a revised version of a piece that first appeared in *Jazz Connection*, Book 2.

As the title suggests, the rhythms in this piece are characteristic of the music used for the tango, a popular dance originating in South America. There are two main sections in this piece. The first (mm. 5-20) is the "Tango" section. It is in the key of D Minor and features chords common to the Latin jazz style. The second section (mm. 21-32) is the "Blues" section. It switches to F Major (the relative major of D Minor), and is a modified 12-bar blues. The melody contains a descending blues figure, yet its rhythms still evoke the tango. For full dramatic effect this piece should be played briskly with great confidence and passion.

Bossa Rio
Use after JPB2.
This piece first appeared in *Jazz Connection*, Book 3.

South American jazz also inspired this brisk and syncopated finale (to be played with straight eighth notes). Each section contains unique technical challenges. The first section (m.5) uses a rhythmic bass figure seen in both "Out on a Limbo" and "Island Breeze." This figure should remain steady and supportive against the right-hand melody. The second section (m.21) features a series of leaping left-hand broken chords. Despite the varying shapes, the rhythm remains the same. Focus on the left hand until you can play these figures "by feel," with only the slightest glimpses to reposition your hand. The melody moves to the left hand in the third section (m.37)—play it clearly and confidently as the right hand plays light, steady chords throughout.